Irma Bohmer came to England in 1958 to learn English. Initially this was for 12 months. Seeing the white cliffs of Dover from the ferry, she felt welcome. After one year and some evening classes, her reading was adequate, but her conversation needed more practice. So she stayed on, married and had two children. Now she knew that this was the country she wanted to live in. She continued her education at London University and felt confident about her English. But she shied away from Shakespeare as this demanded a skill she thought she did not have yet. Then she heard about Sam Wanamaker's idea to build a Shakespeare Globe Theatre. There was an opportunity to volunteer at this project and she did. This was a good introduction to Shakespeare's language and his plays. A bonus was an introduction to English history which she had not studied yet. Volunteering at The Globe became a passion which continues to this day.

To many people I met at The Globe who made my time there so enjoyable.

Irma Bohmer

NEVER MIND SHAKESPEARE

AUSTIN MACAULEY PUBLISHERS™

LONDON • CAMBRIDGE • NEW YORK • SHARJAH

A CIP catalogue record for this title is available from the British Library.

ISBN 9781528938358 (Paperback)
ISBN 9781528969512 (ePub e-book)

www.austinmacauley.com

First Published (2020)
Austin Macauley Publishers Ltd
25 Canada Square
Canary Wharf
London
E14 5LQ

Table of Contents

Introduction

My education in Germany started in a small, catholic, village-school. It was very basic. The girls were taught by women and the boys by men. The buildings were separated by a 10-minute walk. It was just after the war. Most of the male teachers had to join the army and their wives took their place. I do not know if they were qualified, and of course, usually female teachers were not allowed to marry. The hours of our education were cut as part of the building had to be used for the education of the refugees. They were of a different religion and could not join our classes.

As I was an only child and lived on a farm, I only came in contact with other children at the school. I loved school. I had learned to read, an activity that one can do alone. The books we used were provided for me, as my father was killed in the war and I was called a war-orphan. One thing that annoyed me was that I had to return these books at the end of each year. I could never find enough material to read and used to pester anyone who might have something to lend me.

The village school finished at primary level and we could go to the next school in the nearby town. My mother relied heavily on her brothers to give guidance with my up-bringing. Two girls from my class had extra tuition to enter university and I begged my mother to let me join them. The state would have paid for me again, as I was a war-orphan. My uncles decided that this was not a good idea. As a girl, I would marry and bring up a family and extra education was a waste of time.

I loved school very much and from the age of about seven, I had already made up my mind to be a teacher. I could think of nothing more enjoyable then to spend all day in a school.

When we were given three titles for a story to write, I did all three. This was just for the pleasure of it.

One of our teachers, briefly, started a class to teach English, and of course, I asked to join. We learned the prayer in English and started every lesson with this. That was as far as it went. One day the teacher suggested that perhaps learning English was not for me. I had not made much progress. Then as now, I do not like to be told that I am not capable of doing something. I never forgot her remark.

So, my education ended and I worked in a local shop. Village life, for me, was much too restricted and I could not wait to leave. I moved to the city of Munster. I took my driving test and became a delivery person. Munster had been bombed heavily and a large part of the city was occupied by the British Army. They lived in identical three-bed-room houses with a small bit of grass in front, maintained by the army. They had their own shops and cinema. I heard English spoken and the remark of my teacher came back to me.

Once again, I had the wish to learn English. I got to know an English family and offered to baby-sit for them. I mentioned my wish to learn English and visit England. I was told that this was no problem. Suddenly, a whole new world opened up for me.

There was an organisation in Germany that helped young people to go and work in England. They would find families that were willing to pay the fare, in return for living with them, looking after their children and doing some housework. It did not take me long to contact them. I was sent forms to fill in. All that was needed was a certificate that I was healthy, a report from the police that I had no conviction and the signature from my mother, as I was only 18 years old. I managed all this almost immediately. I was sent a profile of a family in London, as that was where I wanted to go. There was no haste on their side and the organisation said I did not have to take the first offer. But I did not want to wait, so I accepted. I got in touch with the family and was told that they had a three-year-old boy. They sent me a ticket to London and I made preparations to go. I was so excited that I did not think of the worry I would cause my mother.

On 18th November 1958, I boarded a train in Munster and was on my way to London. I did not have much luggage, as I had forwarded all my books. I had more books than clothes.

The train journey was during the night, but I was too excited to sleep. The ferry trip was great. The weather was sunny and when I saw the White Cliffs of Dover, I felt like I was coming home. We had another medical check-up in Dover. Things were really strict in those days. We had signed a 12-month working permit and had to live-in during that time. If we got into trouble or pregnant, we would be sent back home straight away.

I had sent a photograph of me to the family and they recognised me when I arrived at Victoria. Then it occurred to me that I should have checked if they spoke German. Luckily for me, they did, apart from the little boy. The family lived near Cricklewood in a semi-detached house. All that was of no importance to me. I was in England. The family was very kind. They took me to all the places I needed to go to and sign more forms. The little boy helped me very much in learning English. I enrolled at the Polytechnic and started to learn English. It was much easier and all the other students were at the same level as me. The television programmes went over my head, and it took a while for me to join in the laughter.

On my first free afternoon, I went to Oxford Street. I took the bus and felt very proud of myself for managing. In one shop I saw a display of books. There was a pile of 'The Complete Works of Shakespeare'. I bought a copy and carried it around all afternoon. I still have that copy.

After one year at the Polytechnic, I took the Cambridge Certificate of English Language and passed. I had worked so hard with reading and always carried a dictionary with me. I also made many lists of words and memorised them. After one year, I felt that my conversation still needed practice. I applied for another 12-month permit. As housework was not my favourite occupation, I thought of doing something else. Of course, it had to be a living-in position. Through the Labour Exchange, I found a place at St. Thomas' Hospital. It was work in the nurses dining room. This gave me more contact with girls from all over the world, but very few English people. We all wanted to meet English people to practise the language, but that proved to be the hardest part.

In 1969, I was accepted at London University, but I had to take an English test first. I passed this. One thing I shall not forget is the dictation test. One of the words was 'quaint' and I had never heard it before. I got it wrong, but the rest was fine and I had my place. I read Philosophy and Music and got my degree in 1973. While at college, the drama department talked and presented many of Shakespeare's plays and he became more familiar to me. I finally had the courage to go see his plays at some of the London Theatres.

When I left college, I decided to teach. I read the Times Educational Supplement every week. In 1995, there was a small notice in it asking for volunteers to the Globe Theatre. I had not heard anything about this, but it appealed to me and I contacted them. A group of 39 people met in an old building in Bear Gardens. There was an enormous bear in the entrance room. Most of the people there, had been involved with the creation of the Globe. Sam Wanamaker, the American actor, had campaigned for this building. It took a lot of effort to get the permission from Southwark Council. So many of the people at the first meeting knew a lot about it and I sat quietly at the back, listening. It sounded like such an exciting idea.

We were given a brief history of the original Globe Theatre. The present building was not quite finished as there was
no grant to help with the cost. It needed sponsors and volunteers. The people in charge were trying out a number of ways
of dealing with this new venture. There were many decisions

to make. We all signed up. The question of tourists arose and if we spoke a foreign language then this would be useful too.

The first artistic director was appointed. It was Mark Rylance. As an actor, he had many ideas on how to treat this theatre. It was decided to start this unfinished theatre with four weeks of workshops. The new Globe was like a child and we would be involved in helping it grow. It was all experimental and there were frequent changes. What should the stewards wear? Initially, it was black clothes and we were given a blue sash to make us visible to the audience. We wore a chain with our name and photograph on it and I was very proud of this.

I could not wait to get started. In 1995, it was still possible to drive to London. Parking at weekends was easy and it took me about 20 minutes get there.

Mark knew what he wanted to do from an actor's point of view. The stage was meant to be as it was, without amplification, extra lights or many props. The yard was for standing and the price was £5. Mark's wife, Claire van Kampen, a musician, was dealing with music in the Elizabethan times. There was an orchestra which used original instruments. On several Sundays, there were concerts, but the audience was very small.

Pre-Season

The pre-season started on Wednesday, 9th August 1995. There were two ticket prices, £5 for standing in the yard and £11 for sitting. The theatre was not finished and the lower parts were only used for sitting. Many actors came to the workshops, as they were keen to find out about this new place. The pillars on the stage were square ply-wood and gave rise to much conversation. Was it possible to work around these? Many people from the audience were keen to go onto the stage and it was our duty to prevent this. Others were also eager to walk around the piazza where the building materials were stacked and we had to discourage them stepping over the stones.

My first duty was on Saturday, 12th August. I was working full-time and could only come on weekends. The workshop was Tony Butler speaking about 'Realising Images—Listening, Hearing and Feeling Images'. On Sunday 13th, Bill Bryden and William Dudley talked about 'The Miracle Plays and Shakespeare'. On Sunday 20th, Richard Griffiths gave us 'The Boring Bits of the Dream'. On 2nd September, Yvonne Brewster showed us 'Balconies and Hiding Places'. My last duty that year was on the 3rd with Ian Judge's 'Shakespeare and the Daylight Audience'.

These talks covered a range of possibilities and opportunities that the Globe could offer. The events were informative, but the subjects were new to me. I got an insight on how to look at a play and how actors use a space. This was a whole new world to me and I loved it. Many local people came to see the progress of this venture. After all, it was the first building in our times that had a thatched roof. The concession made, was that it had to have sprinklers. The area was run-down and had a few eating places. The walk along the river was basic and not many tourists ventured there. The interest was mixed, positive and negative. A frequent comment from visiting actors was 'This will never work'.

As stewards, we became very knowledgeable about buildings and their construction in the Elizabethan times. This was something, again, that I did not know anything about. My education had not dealt with English History and I was trying hard to catch up. The weather was typically English and I do not remember any bad days. That may be because I was totally committed to this venture. I had not yet seen a Shakespeare play, but I had gained much background information. It had also been a good introduction into audience behaviour.

The season had been short and the people in charge at the Globe gained much experience on how to proceed. As a music teacher, the autumn term was busy to get ready for Christmas. So, I put Shakespeare on hold.

To my surprise and delight, I received a letter from the Globe in January 1996. It asked if I would be interested to steward again this year. Of course, I would. The people at the Globe had had some time to think how things would go, now that they had some experiences gathered during the previous year. The play was 'The Two Gentlemen of Verona'. One of the actors was a dog called Denis. He had his dressing-room (kennel) on the top terrace. His 'Good luck cards' were pinned there. He knew his cue and performed perfectly to the delight of the audience.

The stewards came together on 12th August. We were given a tabard to wear over our black garments. They had writing on the front and back and a large pocket. It made us visible from all directions and we loved them.

I stewarded on 24th August and saw my first Shakespeare play. To my delight, the language was understandable to me. I worked a few more Sundays. On 3rd September, the Northern Broadsides gave a performance of 'A Midsummer Night's Dream' under Barrie Rutter. The price for the yard tickets was one penny as it had been in Elizabethan times. As it was the first day of the new term, I had to miss this. I do not like to miss out and I bored my colleagues with the talk about stewarding at the Globe. It became obvious now, that we would be a permanent part and I was delighted about this. It felt unique, at least to me, and I was so pleased to be there.

The Theatre

Nobody really knows what the first Globe looked like. This reconstruction is made as faithful as it can be. It is about 200 yards from the original position. There is a building there, and our Globe was built as near as possible. There is a plaque where the old Globe used to be and visitors often walk there and take photographs. The Rose Theatre is near it. When our Globe was created the techniques used were painstakingly accurate. 'Green' oak was cut and lime plaster was mixed according to a contemporary recipe.

There are concessions to the 21st century. The thatched roof has sprinklers in it. There are illuminated signs, extra exits, fire-retarded materials and machinery backstage.

The seats are wooden benches and apart from the back row, there are no backs to them. To make it more comfortable to the modern audience, there are cushions and seatbacks for hire. The Gentlemen's Boxes are in the Middle Gallery and have chairs with cushions. Box 'P' is used for wheelchair patrons as this is nearest to the lift. The boxes seat 10, and the view is from the side. However, the feeling is intimate and very comfortable. I often brought a friend, who is in a wheelchair and she was so pleased to watch Shakespeare from there.

At the start of the Globe, there were no extensions to the stage. Mark Rylance liked to use the stage as it was. When Dominic Dromgoole became Artistic Director, he experimented with extensions into the yard and this made it interesting for the groundlings. They had more spaces to rest their elbows. There were changes again when Emma Rice was Artistic Director. During one play there were tables with table cloth in the yard and the actors jumped from one of these to another table.

The yard was also used by the actors for entries and exits to and from the stage. They fought their way through the Groundlings in the yard. The punters loved this and so did most of the actors. Occasionally, there were carts wheeled through the crowd and it is surprising to see how easy it is to make room in a filled place.

The tickets for standing in the yard have been £5 since the opening of the Globe. The yard is also the best place to be near the actors. The audience can walk about during the performance. It is also useful to get out of the sun or to find more shelter when it rains.

The performances do not stop when it rains. We sell plastic macs, and the stewards also wear them. It is great to see the audience stay during a storm, (umbrellas cannot be opened) and still enjoy the play.

There was a performance of 'Titus Andronicus' when the yard was covered with large strips of cloths. Lucy Bailey was the producer. There was a different atmosphere in the place. One day it rained, and the water build up in the material. Then there was a gust of wind and the cloth moved and emptied the water on the people standing underneath. Most saw the funny side of it. We did.

The Gates

Sam Wanamaker's wish for the Globe had been that it should be an 'Arts Centre', a place that would bring people of all ages and nationalities together. Unfortunately, he died and never saw his vision come to life.

The Globe architect, Theo Crosby, had an idea for decorative iron gates. This would be the entrance from the river to the theatre. He approached Richard Quinnell, a metalworker, in 1989. Theo had an idea about a gate. They focused on birds, animals, insects and flowers from Shakespeare's plays and sonnets. Then they decided to invite blacksmiths from England and abroad to make these motifs. Sadly, Theo died, and did not see the finished product. 125 motifs were created by amateur and professional blacksmiths from all over the globe. One hundred and thirty blacksmiths from 12 nations donated their work. The youngest was a 12-year-old from Australia. Brian Russell and his team forged the gates. These, and the motifs were then rust-proofed and painted.

On 19th and 20th April 1997, 80 blacksmiths from around the world watched the hanging of the gates and the forging of the motifs. The 'Forge-in' was organised by and sponsored by The Ford Motor Company. On 12th June 1997, the Chairman, Sir Alex Trotman, commanded the gates to be opened officially for the first time, to admit Her Majesty, the Queen and His Royal Highness, the Duke of Edinburgh. It was the celebration marking the opening of the Globe Theatre. Iron Gates were rare in Elizabethan Times. So, there was no problem to make them authentic.

The gates are impressive. The Groundlings who queue there are admitted through them before any of the other doors open. They are also a much- photographed item. Many brides have their day made special by having their pictures taken there. Another interesting activity is to work out which motif comes from which of Shakespeare's plays or sonnets.

The Opening of the Globe

1997 was the official opening of Shakespeare's Globe Theatre in London. The people involved in the running of this place now had a clearer idea of how to use it. Just like the growing up of a child, this is an ongoing process. The Globe Theatre was now in teenage mode.

The Queen and Prince Philip arrived by barge on 12th June. They entered through the Groundling Gates. The play was 'Henry V'. The season had started in May and would run until September. It was a workday for me and once again, I missed something I would have liked to take a part in.

The Shakespeare plays that year were 'Henry V' and 'The Winter's Tale'. There were two plays by contemporary authors, 'A Chaste Maid in Cheapside', by Thomas Middleton, and 'The Maid's Tragedy', by Francis Beaumont and John Fletcher.

Each year, a foreign company played at the Globe for one week. In 1997, it was Umabatha who performed 'Macbeth' in Zulu. It was impressive and I felt so privileged to be able to steward this. I do not know if I would have booked tickets for this play. Not only was it a Shakespeare play but this was yet another language that I could not understand. Seeing the play, though, made no difference as I knew the story.

The Stewards

It was now obvious that the stewards were going to be a permanent fixture at the Globe. We were growing with the place. Each year when we returned after the winter break, there were changes. The theatre was now finished, but the surroundings were not. In the beginning, the actors' dressing rooms were in porta cabins and a steward had to be there. If it rained, then we could shelter in the toilets. The actors were most kind and cared about us.

At the beginning of the season, we usually had a welcome party. Food was arranged by several people and it often took place in the steward's room. This also changed each year, as the space was needed for other activities. When we did come back the steward's room was often in a different place. This gave us a good knowledge of the building. We did get to know the complexities of it. As I was working full time, I could only come on weekends. During the week, I bored my friends and work colleagues by talking about the exciting things that happened at the Globe.

The theatre was open to the elements and it did sometimes rain and was often cold. It was up to us to dress appropriately. It was our first duty to make the audience welcome and help them enjoy the play. Of course, we could also watch the plays, but that was our second consideration.

The seats in the Globe were wooden benches, apart from the Gentlemen's Rooms. We hired cushions for £1 to make it more comfortable. The Gentlemen's Rooms had cushions already. The position on the cushion cart was outside the theatre and open to the elements. I did like this position, and these stewards were the first people, that members of the audience came in contact with. It was important to make them welcome without being too officious. A visit to the Globe, at the beginning, was as new to them as it was to us being there.

Sainsbury's sponsored the cushions for the first two years. The covers needed to be washed at the end of every season and then zipped back. During the first few years, a group of us also came before the season and washed and cleaned the seats.

The yard was a popular place to watch the plays from. Our licence meant that we could stand 700 people. Unfortunately, they were not allowed to sit during the performance as this would have breached our licence. Southwark Council did surprise spot checks. They also made sure that the Gallery doors were shut.

As the Globe had a thatched roof, safety was important. I am pleased to say that during the 25 years I was there, we had an excellent safety record. It also meant that the stairs leading to the seats had to be kept free, and, some audience members did not see why they could not sit or stand there.

The Globe cared very much for our comfort. We were given regular tea-breaks. Biscuits and tea and coffee were available. Each position had two stewards, but when one was on a break there was only one left. This was changed after some years and stewards from an outside position came to give a break. The original policy was that duties were arranged alternatively, one duty in, one duty out. This made it fairer, all round. After all, our place was to make the audience welcome first and seeing the play was a bonus.

Before the last performance, there was the end-of-season party. This took place in the theatre. The tables with food were put on the stage. The stewards, actors, and staff from the various departments were all invited. In 1997, we had Denis, a dog, who was acting in a play. He was also invited to the party and most stewards made a fuss of him. His handler was not pleased when we tried to feed him titbits. Just before the last performance, there was a photograph taken of the stewards and Front of House staff, who had looked after us. From 2005, they listed all the names of the stewards and the year they had started to volunteer, at the end of each programme.

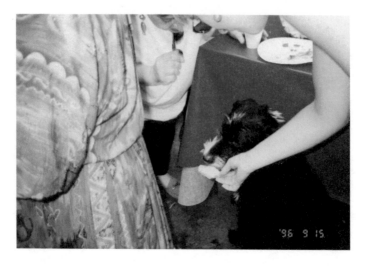

'96 9 15

Standing in the yard was a favourite position for us. Most of the stewards booked a ticket for the first and last performance of each play. They formed a queue outside the Groundling Gates, as these were opened first. The Groundlings made sure that they were standing in their favourite place, immediately before the actors. For the last performance, many stewards bought roses. The thorns had been carefully removed by willing helpers in the stewards' room. These flowers were thrown to the actors after the first curtain call, and the actors often threw them back.

The winter months were a rest for us stewards, but the theatre did not sleep. Students came from all over the world to work on the stage. The décor of the theatre was improved. In the early days, some of us came with mops and brushes and really cleaned the seating.

Each year also brought changes, as the space was allocated differently. The stewards' room needed more lockers, as our numbers grew. The Underglobe was turned into an Exhibition area. The shop needed more space for their extensive merchandise. The FOH needed more room.

As the audiences grew, the number of stewards increased. At the beginning of each new season, it was always interesting to see who had come back and who had not. As there were no stewards from my area in Kent, I did not see anyone during the winter months. As a music teacher, this was welcome. The schools usually started their autumn term with preparation for Christmas.

Right from the beginning, I felt that our position as volunteer at the Globe was unique. Years later, other organisations modelled this format for their place. We had many perks at the Globe. There was always a room with seating and refreshments. Lockers were provided to keep our belongings safe. We wore a special uniform which, at first, was a tabard to keep with the Elizabethan theme. These provided a pocket, to take items we liked to have with us. I liked to keep a book or puzzle handy if I was on an outside position. After some time, we were provided with red aprons. Some of us were nostalgic about the loss of the tabards. I spent many evenings after the performance and checked the pockets for contents. It was interesting to see what was left behind, and sometimes never claimed.

We were usually put at a different position. It was most interesting to see the same play from different angles. How this varied the perception of a play. The actors often made small changes. This must have been useful if the same play was playing for months. We received two free-standing tickets, after we had given 10 shifts. The Musician's Gallery over the stage, was not always used. There were some benches put there and stewards and staff at the Globe could book these seats. One got a very different view of the actors and a very good one of the Groundlings. I often took my granddaughter there. She still remembers when Caliban joined her during a gap of his performance. I also brought my friend, who is in a wheelchair, to sit in the Gentlemen's Box. This was closest to the lift, but the view was sideways. The lift could only be operated by FOH staff, but it was helpful to get up to the galleries.

There was no announcement about no photography; signs were by the doors. Not many people took notice of this, and it was part of our job to discourage taking pictures. Because of the open-air feeling of the place, some people forgot that they were indoors. We also had audience members smoking when this was still permitted indoors. The theatre tried to be friendly and at one time, two stewards had to walk across the stage, just before the start of the play. They carried a large board that said 'No Photography' and when flipped over, said 'Thank You'. This usually got a laugh.

In the early days, we made various refreshments and one time, we carried baskets with apple pies. But the theatre became very popular and was usually sold out. To walk through the yard was not easy and this idea was discontinued.

In June I stewarded a midnight performance. This was really different from those during normal hours. The audience was also different. At the end, the stewards were given breakfast, croissant and Bucks Fizz. It was very jolly sitting in the theatre at 4 am after an exciting performance. Getting home was no problem, as I still drove there.

The 95ers

In 2005, the names of the stewards appeared in the programmes with the year of them starting. This was interesting reading. At the induction meeting, there had been 39, but the numbers went down for different reasons. This gave me an idea. I talked to my colleagues about forming a club and celebrating our long line of service. We called ourselves 'The 95ers' as this was when we had started. The idea was to meet once, each year, after the end of a season and talk and share photographs, and interesting occurrences from that year.

Some stewards started a group and went to the theatre. I did not join this group and therefore, did not see any of my colleagues during the off-season.

The idea of meeting at the Globe after the season was a possible one, but finding a date that 22 people could manage was not so easy. We decided to meet in the stewards' room. Everyone would bring some nibbles and drinks. The stewards who could come, enjoyed the occasion. We talked about the season and shared photographs. On fine days, we went to the top terrace and sat in the sun, and of course, took photographs. There was usually too much food and drink. Then a Turkish restaurant opened across the Globe and offered a reduction and we decided to go there a few times.

The number of 95ers dwindled, as most of us were of a certain age. We went to different restaurants and kept up these meetings. We also went for lunch at Middle Temple Hall. Although photographs were not permitted there, the ushers were very friendly and as the Globe had performed there, they allowed us to take a photograph when everyone else had left.

In 2014, we had been stewarding for 20 years and we decided to celebrate this event. Once again, we went to Middle Temple Hall. I had mentioned this to the Theatre Department. To our surprise, they offered to pay for our drinks. We did not abuse this offer. When we arrived at Middle Temple, we were told there was a package for us. I picked it up and put it on a table. "Not there," said the usher. "This is the High Table." We chose our food and enjoyed the meal. Then I opened the parcel and in it were copies of a facsimile from the First Folio of 'The Tragedy of Romeo and Juliet'. I gave everyone a copy and suddenly there was a lot of laughter. Each copy had been signed by Neil Constable, Dominic Dromgoole and Patrick Spottiswoode. It also had our names on the title page. We merrily exchanged our copies with the one which had our name in it. As we had now done 20 years, we discussed if we should call an end to this. There were only a few of us left and it seemed a good time to stop. I even thought of giving up stewarding at the Globe, but then I knew I would miss it too much. It had become my 3rd job and I continued coming.

There were now quite a few stewards who had done a long service, but we decided that we would remain 'The 95er'. We talked occasionally of going out again for a meal, but it never gave us that enthusiasm we had started with. Other stewards had formed interest groups and these flourished. I did not join any. A medal was given each year to a person who had given much to the Globe. The executive members decided to give it to the stewards who had given their time for 20 years and more. This, of course, included the 95ers. We all stood on the stage, were given a medal and had our photograph taken. There were speeches. I had found a tabard, and decided to wear this in memory of my long service.

There was one more surprise. I was asked if I would like to go to the Tea Party at Buckingham Palace. Well, of course, I would like to. My family are spread out over Europe and I went with Sylvia Chinoy. It was 72 degrees, which was a sunny, but cold day and we had a good time. We were told that The Duke of Edinburgh would like to speak to us. The equerries kept us in order. We enjoyed the day. The dress code was interesting and varied. I watched with amusement as some people tried to pull their stiletto heels out of the ground. The gardens were looking good and many of us walked and admired the plants.

So, my 20 years at the Globe had gone. How many more will I be able to do? I know, I will only stop if my body tells me I cannot do this. Standing for three hours has been easy so far.

The Stewards Room

The stewards' room has moved a lot over the years. As the building work progressed, we had to make room for other offices. This was no problem when there were just a few of us. But now there are over 600 volunteers. We are not all there at the same time, but it can get very crowded in the summer. This summer, we had many education events in the SWP and two performances in the theatre. Sometimes, there were education events in the Nancy Knowles Theatre as well. Luckily, we have an outside seating area and this helps in the good weather. We can also use the piazza.

When we had a room above the place we are in now, we could sit on the top terrace. The view is amazing. In 2000, we were allowed to watch the fireworks from there. Now that space is the Front of House office, the doors need a pass and us ordinary stewards have not got that. I miss that place, as it was so quiet there, and I like to read if there is a long gap between shows.

The FOH people look very well after us. They are the ones who stay, well after we have gone home. In my earlier days, I used to help checking tabard pockets for forgotten items, fold rain macs and help generally with clearing up. We have a table now, and some very comfortable chairs. These were a gift from somewhere and not very clean. I came in one morning and washed the chairs. It made it look neater. This space was perhaps, almost my second home.

Some stewards stayed on Sundays and relaxed on the piazza. I am always running for the train so that I can get home before midnight.

Now the Globe is fund raising for further building work. The place is getting too small for all the events that are taking place there now. Where will we end up next? Perhaps there will be a purpose-build stewards' room with all mod cons? I cannot wait.

There are still a few of us 95ers left. Each year, I think perhaps I should stop while I still enjoy it. But I would miss it too much. It is the place with its history and our seeing it grow and contributing to that growth. There is a loyalty we feel about this place that has given us so much. I cannot imagine a time when I will not be coming to the Globe. It has been my home, literally sometimes, and also my third job.

Animals at the Globe

The Globe is an outdoor theatre and like all outsides, animals come and go. In the Globe the audience could bring in food, as long as it was not in glass. Some punters held picnics during the interval. We all know if there is food, there is wildlife. It did not take the pigeons long to become aware of this new eating place. They were not shy of people and provided additional entertainment. Some actors included them in their performance to the delight of the groundlings.

The original Globe had a yard that had hazelnuts shells. This was tried, but the birds ruined it. And during the winter, the place was not busy and so, was available to other life. I remember doing my first shift. There was a pigeon perching on the roof over the stage. The yard was crowded and the bird moved its head from side to side. It appeared to say: What has happened to this place and who are all those people?

During one season, the play 'Love's Labour's Lost', ended with a mock fight using baguettes. The message soon went around the bird world. They did not even wait for the audience to leave. They descended straight after the curtain call.

Then we had a blackbird making a nest in the Upper Gallery. It hatched one young. This little one used to sit at the edge of Gentlemen's Box P and chirp. The mother answered and brought food. The actors had lost their audience for a while. Unfortunately, there was mess under the nest and this was not on at the Globe. So, some netting was put in the area and we did not see the bird again.

I have already mentioned Denis the dog, who had his kennel at the upper terrace. Then we had some chickens there, and they became very friendly. As soon as one stepped near them, they came to the fence. They had a short part in a market scene, being carried across the stage. They even provided eggs.

Then we had a live snake in 'Antony and Cleopatra'. I often wondered if the looks and actions of the actress were real fright or very good acting. The snake escaped and was not used again. Then there was Washington who came to the stage on a real horse. The horse had no trouble going up into the piazza, but it was not so easy going down at the end of his act. I also wondered about the actor, was he happy riding for 5 minutes before each performance? The horse did not come cheap.

Then there was a King Charles Cavalier in 'Nell Gwynn'. She was a delight (the dog), and loved going for walks on the piazza. We all made a fuss of her, and it made her day. The non-acting animals are the mice. With left-over food all over the place they are doing well. It is impossible to remove small crumps and that is, of course, a meal for such a small animal. I often see them scampering across the Southbank when I make my way to the station. I know it is not the same one and I christened him/her Hamlet. I even saw one when we were at Middle Temple Hall. It appeared from under the hired seating. I was wondering if someone would scream and as I was stewarding, what would I do?

The Globe encourages people with disabilities to come to plays and we have stewards who are very good in looking after their dogs and it is a cherished position with the stewards.

The Audience

The audience is another interesting part of the Globe. They are fascinating to watch and they change with every performance. In the pre-season, the yard was not always full and there was an opportunity to walk around and watch them from different angles. It also gave stewards a change of view of an often-watched play. In the early days, a steward would walk in the yard with a basket of 'Elizabethan Apple pies', for sale. But when the theatre sold out, this has not been possible any more. The audience can eat and drink and have picnics, as long as they do not bring glass. This would not be safe on the stone floor. There are few restrictions and people can come in and out during the performance, even when the play has started. This may be disturbing to those people sitting near the doors. But it has been the policy from the start. It also helps audience members whose feet hurt, to go out for a little while and then come back again.

Photographs are allowed, as long as no actors and musicians are on the stage. The audience can sit on the floor during the in-coming and the interval, but not during the play. This is a licence issue. We have 700 standing places. This is reduced if the stage is extended. It would be reduced if sitting during the play would be permitted. Southwark Council do unexpected checks to ensure that the doors in the galleries are shut during the play and that the stairs to the seats are kept clear of bags and people. This is a safety precaution. During my time, there have only been three evacuations. Once a person walking along the river saw smoke coming out of the theatre and called the fire brigade. They came very quickly and saw the bright side of it when it turned out to be dry ice. Another time, someone lit a barbecue nearby and sprinklers started to work.

They were very efficient and poured a lot of water into the theatre.

Occasionally, audience members feel unwell. Some of the stewards are Globe designated First Aiders (FA). We deal initial with this matter and have a fireman who will then take over and, if necessary, take people to the first aid room. There is a First Aider on every level. Sometimes people forget to eat and drink and think that standing for a few hours is fine. When we take them for a lie down in the first aid room, they usually recover quickly and return to the play. In this age of mobiles, we sometimes get an audience member dialling 999. This is not necessary and we look well after our visitors. Many are appreciative and we get many thank-you letters. The play usually continues, unless there is much disruption. When Mark was on the stage, he used to judge the situation. If he thought a pause was needed, he indicated this with his little finger. The actors then paused until the little finger gave the go-on sign.

Mark Rylance thought the yard was the stomach of the place, the source of the appetite. The lower and Middle Galleries were the heart, intent on emotion. The Upper Gallery was the mind, where the wit was most appreciated of all.

There have been many interesting comments over the years. Most have made us laugh. During a very hot spell someone asked me if the theatre was air-conditioned. I enjoy replying: "Yes, there is a hole in the roof." Our aim is to make visitors welcome, to enjoy their visit and perhaps come back. We remain polite and most people respond. There have, of course, been a few occasions when it was hard. There was only one time when it was really difficult for me to remain cool and calm. An audience member was sitting on the stairs during the play, and, after asking if she was alright, I had to tell her to stand or to go out for a little while. She did so. During the interval, a person sitting near these stairs, admonished me for telling someone who was, perhaps, unwell to stand up. I tried to explain the reason, but she would not accept anything and continued to argue. She ended with a final remark: "At least I am English." I am not often speechless, but this time I was and I could not think of an answer. I mentioned this to

Front of House and did not want this to go further. I am a foreigner and have an accent. This stayed in my mind and I am glad it was the only one that upset me very much.

During my time as a teacher, we adopted a toy dog, a Shar Pei and the children called him Rover. They could take him on journeys and on holidays and then report back with stories and photographs. Well, I took Rover to the Globe, and he made friends with the Front of House and had his photograph taken in the theatre. Sometimes, we get guide dogs who come with their owners and there are many stewards who ask to be a dog steward.

The Education Department

Sam Wanamaker was very keen on developing the education part of the Globe. The space in Bear Gardens was very small and therefore, could only hold a few students. When the building work started on the Sackler, education events had to move to the Globe. The part that was going to be the Sam Wanamaker Playhouse was on three levels and was known as 'Inigo Jones 1, 2 and 3'. Then there was the Nancy Knowles Theatre, which could also be used. Demands for these places were great and had to be carefully scheduled.

Patrick Spottiswoode came to the department in 1984 and became Director of Education in 1989. He is still there and is the longest serving member connected with the Globe. He initiated so many events. Most of these took place during the day and as I was still working full-time, I could only steward them occasionally. Once I retired, I enjoyed that side of the Globe very much. I was always keen in learning more.

Patrick started the 'Read not Dead', performances. It was plays that were rarely performed. A group of actors would rehearse on one morning, usually a Saturday or Sunday. They then read the plays in the afternoon in the Nancy Knowles Theatre. Most of the time, there was an introduction session before. The audience was like a club and they knew so much about those authors and enjoyed the productions immensely. There was usually a rush of stewards volunteering for this, as we could sit in during them. I was back to not knowing and trying to keep up.

The friends of the Globe had a 'Meeting the Cast' of the current play. Most of the actors came into the Nancy Knowles Theatre and the friends could ask questions. The event ended with a drink and further talks. There was also a 'Question and

Answer' session when the public could buy a ticket and ask questions of two or three actors.

During the early days of the Globe, there were sessions on Saturdays for children whose parents were in the audience. Globe workers took the children through the highlights of the play with movement and art. Then the children went into the theatre for the final part of the play. I liked these sessions and used many ideas with my class. Some of the parents took their children there, after I mentioned it.

There were study days, when Globe practitioners and university lecturers came for the day and gave lectures and workshops, on a particular Shakespeare play. This was very interesting for me as I could sit in during these events and I learned a lot about the backgrounds of the Shakespeare plays. During the school holidays, there was story-telling for the youngsters, some for very young children who came with their parents. These were a kind of play with audience participation. They also took place in the NKT.

Many students came from abroad to work on theatre skills. These were run by Globe practitioners and actors. Once the Globe season had ended for the year they could perform on the stage, although it was cold then. Stewards were also needed for this. We were very critical and looked for prospective actors who might come to the Globe one day.

The Globe also provides an MA course on Shakespeare, in conjunction with King's College. I would have liked to take this, but it was always on a Thursday and that was not a day I could manage.

In the spring of 2011, The Education gave a whole term of events on 'Shakespeare is German'. As usual, I could not resist and stewarded most of those talks. Shakespeare is on the curriculum in nearly all the schools in Germany now. How I wish it had been during my time, but perhaps the village schools would never have done it. I bought a ticket for those sessions that did not need a steward. We went on a visit to the Goethe Institute. We also saw a very old film, at the British Film Institute. It was interesting to see how such a film still had merits. We had a talk about translating Shakespeare into

German by Frank Gunther. He explained that one cannot translate by word, but needs to consider the meaning. He said that he often sat for hours contemplating a sentence. I knew, I would not attempt such a feat. When I went to the European Bookshop in Piccadilly, sometime afterwards, I found some of his translations and bought a few, just to see what he had done.

One year, (I cannot remember when), the Education Department decorated the top room at the Sackler and made it into a fairy grotto with Christmas ideas. It was magical and the children from three upwards, whatever, enjoyed it tremendously. It was sad to hear that it could not be repeated the year after.

As stewards, we were not really involved with the Exhibition. A few times, they put on events where the parents could bring their children to take part in activities. Then we were needed. One was when they tried something called 'Frost fair'. I was disappointed, as I had researched this topic at Somerset House and had expected great things. But that was me being over-enthusiastic.

There was one very exciting event in the Exhibition every year during the Christmas Season. We dispensed 'Mulled Wine' to those people who came for a tour of the Globe Theatre. Shirley, who was a Globe volunteer, knew a lot about Elizabethan recipes. She made her own spices and the whole building smelled delicious. Every person on the tour got a small cup of hot mulled wine. Shirley was explaining and stirring a large saucepan. That was a real treat for some of us. I offered my services well in advance, as did a few others.

The season at the Globe tended to start in May, but was brought forward to April, if possible, on Shakespeare's birthday. The Globe and the exhibition had a free day with multi activities. I only remember the sunny days and the place was heaving. People could go onto the stage and proclaim their favourite saying. It was a long day for all of us and it was surprising to me how many people had never been to the Globe.

Mark started Sonnet Walks. These began at a place that had connections with the Bard. People booked a place, were given a rose and a sheet of instructions, and went on a walk. Stewards stood at strategic place to make sure they were on the right track.

At certain places, an actor would suddenly appear and speak. The walk would end at the Globe and the roses would be put into the Groundling Gate. Some walks started in Shoreditch and some in Westminster. They went on most of the day and on the last walk, the stewards would join and so ended their day at the Globe. The walks were very popular and did take place on the days advertised, even if it rained.

In 2014, Dominic Dromgoole took a group of 12 actors on a two-year world tour. They were going to visit and perform 'Hamlet'. The idea, apparently, came up during a relaxed session in the bar. Where else? They did not take stewards, unfortunately.

In 2016, Dominic gave us 'The complete walk'. Screens were put up between St. Thomas Hospital Gardens and Potters Fields Park. They showed scenes from all 37 plays. Stewards were placed at various places. This happened on Saturday 23rd April and Sunday 24th April. I remember it being a dry day.

Deutsche Bank sponsors Shakespeare productions for schools. This takes place in March, before the season starts. The weather is, as is usually during that time of year variable. Some days are sunny and dry, others are wet, and occasionally we have snow. The performances last one and a half hour, without an interval. The local schools are invited and schools further afield, can pay a small amount. For many of the children, this is a first visit to a Shakespeare play. The teachers have been sent notes to prepare the pupils, but not all the children find it easy to stand in all the weather and listen. However, many are really interested and I enjoy stewarding these events. A few of these performances are later in the day, and on weekends. They encourage parents and grandparents to accompany their children to these family performances. They are very popular and introduce many youngsters to Shakespeare. The stewards have seen changes during these performances. Mobiles are common and talking during a show is also normal. It is hard for older people to accept this chatting, but often the talk is about the action on the stage. Schools usually take a whole class and it is obvious that not all the children take the same interest. But if even one child is gripped by the action on the stage, it is a worthwhile event.

The Plays

I have now been at the Globe for 25 years and have enjoyed my time there very much. Shakespeare has become a friend and as my understanding of his language grew, so did my love for his words. I have seen all his plays, some more than once. There have been productions in many languages.

During the first 10 years, Mark Rylance gave us productions in Elizabethan dress, in modem dress, all male productions, all female productions and a variety of this.

It was exciting and taught me a lot of English History. Then Mark left as he had covered so much and he wanted to do other things. He invited the stewards, who had started with him in 1995, to a farewell party. We know that there would be changes and most of us looked forwards to this. I was ready to have my gaps in Shakespeare knowledge filled.

Often visitors ask what my favourite Shakespeare play is. I cannot really answer this. The productions differ and each one has its merit. There are often actors or scenes that stand out. Sometimes personal memories come during a performance.

In 1997, Umabatha staged Macbeth in Zulu. This showed me that if one knows the story, there is great enjoyment in any language performance. The Merchant of Venice, in 1998, had Norbert Kentrup, acting Shylock. He was the founder of the Bremen Shakespeare Company.

Peter Oswald was writer in residence at the Globe. In 1998-1999, he wrote 'Augustine's Oak', the first commissioned play by Shakespeare's Globe. Vanessa Redgrave played Prospero in 'The Tempest' in 2000. During our end of the season party, we wanted to float balloons. It was raining and they did not float, but Vanessa came up with a good idea.

The foreign company that played that year was 'Grupo Galpao', Brazilian street-artists. They were founded in 1982 and their aim was to bring theatre to people who had not experienced this before. They gave us 'Romeo and Juliet'. There was a Volkswagen as dressing room on the stage. The actors walked on a tight-rope, played the accordion, and used Brazilian songs. Their faces were painted white and red and their costumes were imaginative. Another foreign company that year was 'Kathakali', who gave us 'King Lear' in their language.

Umabatha came back in 2001. Peter Oswald wrote another play for the Globe: 'The Golden Ass', a story based on that by Apuleius. Mark Rylance played Lucius. Liam Brennan was an old woman who told a very long story using puppets. As I had read the book many years before; I really enjoyed the play. In 2003, the Globe showed a play by Christopher Marlowe: 'Dido, Queen of Carthage'. This is really a play designed to be performed by choirboys. The set was a playground on a giant scale and I would have liked to have a go on the slide. This was not permitted. Shame. This was also the year that Mark played Olivia in 'Twelfth Night'. He had the walk of a woman which really worked and people asked if he was on roller skates. 'The Taming of the Shrew', was an all-female production. Kathryn Hunter was Katherina and Janet McTeer was a very good Petruchio. She had the perfect actions and I loved the production. 2004 gave us a production of 'Romeo and Juliet'. Bette Bourne played the nurse and for me, he got it just right. It was one of the best portrayals of this character I have seen and I have seen a lot. Another play that year was 'Measure for Measure'.

Peter Shorey played Mistress Overdone and he was wearing some very smart, very high, red sandals. At the end of the plays run, I asked if I could buy them. Unfortunately, I could not. That was a pity.

During one performance of 'The Midsummer Night's Dream' there had been heavy rain. A puddle had formed on the front of the stage. The actor who plays Pyramus kills himself and takes some time over it. As he came to the wet patch, he changed his words and actions to "I am drowning" and proceeded to swim. The audience loved it and so did we.

Mark's last year was 2005. I brought a group of friends to
see 'Pericles'. One of the us was in a wheelchair and she
thought she would never be able to go to a theatre again. I
booked the Gentlemen's Box P. They all enjoyed the play. I
parked in the Globe's car park. After the play ended, we went

through the stage door and my friend, who was 85 and very alert, was delighted when some of the actors spoke to her.

On 1st January, Mark invited all the stewards, who had started with him in 1995, to tea at the Swan. There were about 40 of us. Mark gave us a signed copy of a book about the Globe. We were a little sad, but he had done the things he wanted to do and was ready for a change. The Globe had grown and was also ready for a change.

Dominic Dromgoole became the second Artistic Director of the Globe. It was inevitable that there would be changes and most of us welcomed these. Dominic liked to extend the stage and build structures into the yard. This did reduce the number of groundling spaces, but it gave them more opportunities to give their elbows a resting place. The Globe is a living theatre and has to move with the times. There were some interesting debates about: 'Would Shakespeare have approved?' We will never know, but we will have fun talking about it.

For Titus Andronicus, the yard was covered with cloth. There were splits in them for Groundlings to put their heads through. The younger audiences loved this, but the stewards were concerned if we would be able to see someone being unwell. There was a lot of stage blood used and many people found this too much to bear. The papers wrote about the number of fainters and then the audience increased because everyone wanted to see the fainters. There was a club of fainters. The play of 2006 that I liked very much was 'In Extremis' by Howard Brenton. It was about the letters that Heloise and Abelard wrote to each other. It dealt with philosophy, one of my favourite subjects. I saw it many times and re-read their correspondences.

In 2007, Deutsche Bank started to sponsor performances for schools. The first one was: 'Much Ado about Nothing'. It was a shortened production. Many youngsters had not been to a theatre and they could not stop talking. As this was a new idea, we had to play it by ear. It involved a lot of preparations from the Education Department. I was in my element. I missed working with children and I stewarded many performances. It was March and very cold. We dressed appropriately, but of course, the children did not. They were also not used to standing, not even for one hour. But most of them enjoyed it.

'We the People', brought a real horse into the theatre. It came up the steps by the Groundling Gates fairly easily, but had trouble going down those steps.

An interesting extension was created in 2007 for 'Love's Labour's Lost'. It was a triangle with the narrow part towards the audience. FOH decided only 20 people could go in safely. A steward had to be there as well. The audience inside had to remain in it until the interval. Many visitors found this fascinating. I spend many duties in it. It was different.

'Che Walker', was an actor and wrote a play 'The Frontline' for 2008. It was about what happens around an underground station in modern London. There were 24 actors who provided a lively scenario that included drugs, prostitution and much else.

There was much talk about Marmite. I never found out if this was an advert for it. 'Timon of Athens' was a play I had not yet seen. When Timon was living in the forest, his body was covered with mud and other stuff. He then ran through the audience to exit the theatre. One of the Groundlings got some of this make-up on her bag and clothing. She objected loudly and asked for compensation. Many people would have been delighted for this souvenir, but she was not.

Another play that I had not seen was 'Troilus & Cressida'. It had a market scene that used live chickens. They lived on the top terrace in a large wire cage. These chickens were very friendly. I used to sit and read up there, during a long break. When the chickens noticed someone came onto the terrace they came to the wire. They also laid eggs. I wondered if they were bored as they were used only briefly during a market scene. 'The New World' by Trevor Griffiths, was about the Life of Thomas Paine.

The Globe season had been extended. It still started on Shakespeare's birthday or near enough. But it now continued into October. There were more plays by Shakespeare and some new plays. In 2010, there was a play about 'Bedlam'. Madness used to provide entertainment and people paid to visit Bethlehem Hospital. This seems cruel to us, but those places needed the money. I watched this play with mixed feelings because of the content. Howard Brenton wrote a play about 'Anne Boleyn'. There was some more English history for me.

From 1st to 3rd January 2011, there was a 'Winter Wassail'. It featured songs and words to banish the darkness of winter. Peter Hamilton Dyer was the guide through medieval Elizabethan and Victorian eras, with music and poetry. The Gabrieli Consort was conducted by Paul McCreesh. It was cold but very enjoyable. The Globe celebrated the 400th anniversary of the King James Bible. A group of actors recited the text from Palm Sunday to Easter Monday. Quite a few people came with their copy and some even insisted in sitting in the same place. But the theatre was not sold out. I was impressed by the actors. The spoke for seven minutes, before the next one started. The part about the word 'begetting' was a real feat. My admiration was for the actress, who did it so competently.

Halfway through the season, they played 'Doctor Faustus' by Christopher Marlow. I had read various versions of this story in Germany and was fascinated by it. I stewarded the performance many times and then bought a DVD so that I could watch it more over the years. And I have.

In 2011, we had four Shakespeare plays and four non-Shakespeare. I have mentioned two already. Then there was 'The God of Soho' by Chris Hannan. It used an ancient theatrical tradition, the deus ex machina (god out of the machine). This was used in ancient Greece. A figure playing a god was lowered onto the stage by a contraption, a machine, so that the hero, or the plot might be saved. Aristotle mentions it in his Poetics. 'The unravelling of the plot, no less than the complication must arise out of the plot itself, it must not be brought about by the deux ex machina'. Philosophy and theatre go well together.

Another exciting event in 2011, was the opening of the Sackler Studios in Bear Gardens. This was really needed, as the theatre wanted more rehearsal space and room for education events. There was an ever-increasing number of students coming from all over the world and they needed more room. There was also a cafe which was run by the Swan and open to the public.

2012 was the year of the Olympics. Dominic had the idea of putting all the 37 plays by Shakespeare on, each in a different language. It must have taken some organising. Each foreign company performed their play two or three times. The opening weekend was on 21st April with 'Venus and Adonis', performed by the Isango Ensemble from Cape Town. Their voices were incredible and enchanted us all. These plays ended on 9th June with an English performance of 'Henry V'. The audiences were amazing. Many came to see and hear their language and meet other people from their country. The atmosphere in the yard was so lively and everybody was friendly. There were subtitles, but only sentences of actions rather than all the words. There was no need of a word-by-word translation. If one knew the play, it could be understood. The companies performing used the theatrical tradition of their country. This gave an interesting view of the plays.

I have mentioned before, that I hate missing things. I signed up for all the plays. I had decided to put everything else on hold and just be at the Globe. It was like a full-time job and I saw every play, some even twice. I was very grateful to the steward co-ordinator at the Globe. She managed to put me in the theatre and I did appreciate it. Of course, as a FA, it was a good idea to be inside. As I came every day, I started to help by setting up the refreshments and tidying up when needed. I was very tired at the end of this marathon of stewarding. There was also a very helpful intern in the theatre department, who supplied me with as many reviews as she could. I filled seven books with these and my colleagues enjoyed reading them.

The rest of that season was Shakespeare in English. We had: Henry V; The Taming of the Shrew; Richard II; Twelfth Night; Hamlet; As you Like it. It is good to be retired to do all this. I had worked over 100 shifts that year. The next year, 2013, had other excitements.

2013 was the 'Season of Plenty'. There were eight Shakespeare plays, five touring productions, three new plays, four international productions, two Tempest, two King Lear, a true Season of Plenty.

The South African 'Venus and Adonis', the Indian 'Tempest', the Georgian 'As you like it' and the Belarusian 'King Lear' came back.

I could not wait to see 'Gabriel', a play by Samuel Adamson. My interest in music is well-known and I had heard that this play was about a trumpet, a valve less kind that was around in 1690s. Alison Balsom played the music of Purcell and Handel beautifully. After her appearance at the Globe, she was heard everywhere. If one tuned to Classic FM she was there and she and her trumpet became well-known. I stewarded as many shifts as I could get.

'Blue Stockings' by Jessica Swale took me right back to my youth. How much had I wanted to go to university and how often was I told that it was not really worthwhile for a girl. During the play, I was with those girls and felt their anger and disappointment that they could not pursue their ambitions.

'The Lightning Child' by Che Walker and Arthur Darvill is a Greek drama. I have seen and read Euripides and other Greek plays. It fitted in with my studies of philosophy. So, these three new plays were so exciting for me and I felt the Globe had given me a special present. That year, Shakespeare had to take a back seat.

The Deutsche Bank play for 2014 was 'The Merchant of Venice'. I felt very cross with the ending. Shylock was forced to become a Christian. Usually he walks off at the end of the play. But this time he remained and was baptised on the stage. He would never have changed his belief. He would rather have died. But that was my opinion.

There were three foreign plays 'All's Well that Ends Well' in Gujarati; 'A Midsummer Night's Dream' in British sign language; 'Punishment without Revenge' by Lope de Vega in Spanish. The last deals with questions of love and honour. 'Hamlet' was touring the world, but they did not take any stewards. Occasional, we heard news about their activities. As we were not really involved, we did not think about it much.

The new plays in 2014 were: 'Pitcairn' by Richard Bean. It dealt with the Mutiny on the Bounty. 'Holy Warriors' by David Eldridge, focused on the Third Crusade. There was another Greek story that told about the Iliad. It is a book I have dipped into many times, but never managed to read from cover to cover. Plays or films about war, I have avoided. There are too many memories. I did steward 'Doctor Scroggy's War', but did not engage with it.

The idea that was hatched in the bar was THE GLOBE TO GLOBE 'HAMLET'. Twelve actors and four stage managers were going to visit 197 countries, to put on a performance of 'Hamlet'. It was going to take two years. The end would be a performance on the Globe stage. How I would have liked to come along, even for a short while, but that would have been extra organisation. They had enough to do as it was.

The 2015 Season of Justice and Mercy

The Globe gave us 'The Merchant of Venice'. I find the ending of this play hard to take. At the end Shylock is asked to give up his belief as a Jew and become a Christian. My understanding of this character is that he would have died rather than change his religion. In many Productions, he walks away with a small case in his hand. But in this production, he was christened and I found this difficult to take.

I saw King John performed at Gray's Inn and it was really special, as they used the natural light and the room became gradually darker. This added to the atmosphere.

Richard II was memorable. It started with a very young Richard, who then walked out down the extended stage and through the audience. I watch plays based on history, with interest, as my education did not include English history. I know, Shakespeare did not always stick to details, but it gives me a good introduction. I can always fill in the gaps.

As a student of philosophy, I have a love of Greek theatre. The Oresteia is made up of three plays, Agamemnon, Libation Bearers and Eumenides. The version at the Globe was presented as a whole. Of course, there were cuts, as this would have otherwise been very long. As the Greek theatres were in the open, so the Globe theatre was an apt place to give this play.

Jessica Swale had given us Blue Stockings and returned with a play about Nell Gwynn. Gugu Mbatha-Raw played the part with exuberance. Then there was the dog. The audience loved it and the dog loved the walks on the piazza. The play moved to the Westend, with a different cast.

Another play I enjoyed very much was 'The Heresy of Love'. It was written by Helen Edmundson and based on a real-life character. She was Sor Juana Ines de la Cruz. She entered a convent and wrote poems and plays. She was known as 'The Tenth Muse'. However, the bishop did not approve of this and it shows how women were thought of, and still are, to some extent nowadays.

The Wonder Season 2016

To celebrate the 400th anniversary of Shakespeare's death, short films of each Shakespeare's plays were shown on screens along the Thames. It was called the Complete Walk and happened on 23rd and 24th April. Stewards were positioned at various points and people could stroll along and watch the giant screens. Dominic Dromgoole and the Globe, produced this with support from the British Council. The weather was fairly good, but it was a long walk of 2.5 miles between Westminster and Tower Bridge. The films lasted 10 minutes and were accessible to all.

In 2016, we had our third Artistic Director at the Globe. It was Emma Rice, the first woman to take up this post. She had some great ideas for this place. There were trees on the piazza and outside the gate. They sparkled in the dark. The theatre had more lights and an amplification system. The stewards got a new uniform, consisting of turquoise t-shirts and pink or turquoise sweat shirts. The first play was 'A Midsummer Night's Dream'. There were three tables with table cloths in the yard and the actors jumped from one of these to the other. The play was full of music and dance and there was a different audience in the yard. We were often greeted with "I am a Globe novice." The yard was full of young people who enjoyed this version of a Shakespeare play. Meow, Meow played Titania and descended on a rope to great applause. There were also some gender changes.

The title 'Cymbeline' was changed to 'Imogen'. The heroine was called Imogen until the 1980s. Then the editors of the Oxford Complete Works argued that earlier printers had mistaken the two n for an m. Therefore the 2016 play, went back to the old spelling.

'The Amazing Story of Adolphus Tips', was written by Michael Malpurgo and Emma Rice. The idea came from historical events while Michael was in Devon. It is about a little girl who lost her cat. She and her family had to leave their farm as the American soldiers were doing their exercises at the coast. It was performed by the Kneehigh Company.

Summer of Love Season 2017

This was Emma's second season. The play to start this year's list was, of course, Romeo and Juliet. It is interesting to see a play that has been produced so many times and still there are productions which offer something new. That makes it so interesting to be a steward at the Globe. Not only are the plays different, but they also look different from different positions. We very rarely work at the same place and it is exciting to come in and find out where we are going to be. There are also supple chances over a run. The audience are not aware of these, but as a steward we are. This is a bonus when doing many shifts of the same play.

Another play that year was 'Tristan & Yseult'. It was performed by the Kneehigh Company. There was much music of all genres, Of course, Wagner was represented with excerpts from Tristan and Isolde. There was 'O Fortuna' by Carl Orff, one of the most memorable pieces for me and I cannot hear it often enough. I once, many years ago, heard and saw a complete performance with illustrations. It was the definite performance for me and I drove home thinking that this was the best day of my life. The Globe play also had music that I did not know and I enjoyed these excerpts. I am always ready to get to know unfamiliar things.

Boudica was written by Tristan Bernays. There are elements of history in this play, but also myth and imagination.

Gina McKee played the 'Queen of the Iceni'. It was a wonderful part of a powerful woman. I enjoyed it very much and it also filled in some gaps in my knowledge of English history.

Nell Gwynn came back with a different cast. Then there was 'Twelfth Night', 'Much Ado about Nothing' and 'King Lear'.

The 2018 Season

Michelle Terry is our second woman Artistic Director. She is an actress and performed at the Globe. This was her first season and she said that not everyone would agree and like what she offered.

At the end of each season, the Globe Theatre get some kind of makeover. This time, the logo was changed. The team working on this thought about a circle. In Henry V, the place is talked about as 'This Wooden O'. But it is not really a circle, it is 20-sided, a polygon. Once the creative team had this concept, they worked on it. Then they thought about wood and so it became the logo. A piece of oak was in the exhibition to show how the Globe was constructed. It was an actual item from the timber that was used to build the Globe. It was carefully sawed to make it 20-sided. They covered it with red ink and rubbed the paper down on it. It worked and showed the grain in detail. That was it. This is now the Globe's logo and appears everywhere, even on the stewards' aprons. I think what pleased me, was that we were given the option of buying our own aprons and I did so, a red one for the Globe and a black one for the Sam Wanamaker Playhouse. It means bringing and taking it home, as we do not have enough lockers to keep one permanently. These aprons are handmade and contain a piece of costume.

'Hamlet' and 'As You Like It' have the same cast. There is gender changing, which is much in the news this year.

The play 'Emilia', was based on the life of Emilia Bassano, the daughter of an Italian court musician. It was written by Morgan Lloyd Malcolm and commissioned by Michelle Terry. Did Emilia have something to do with Shakespeare?

Was she 'the dark lady'? We shall never know. The character was played by three actresses. Emilia published a poetry book called 'Salve Deus Rex' in 1611. It was one of the first printed collections of original poems by an English woman. She needed sponsorship and became the mistress of Baron Hunsdon. She hoped that her poetry would be read by women and men that it would, "Enforce all good Christians and honourable-minded men, to speak reverently of our sex."

Matt Hartley wrote the play 'Eyam', based on true events that took place in the village of Eyam in the 17th century. Matt grew up in a nearby village. The play was right for the Globe, as it invites a direct relationship with the audience. It was a surprise to me as I had never heard about this village. But talking to some audience members, there were many who had heard about it and even more who had visited the place. When the plague came to Eyam in 1665, it tested the bonds of a community. Over 300 people died and their names were recited by an actor at the close of the play. This was a very emotional time and many audience members had tears in their eyes.

The production of 'Two Noble Kinsmen' was only the second time I saw this play.

The stewards ended the season with the usual end-of-season party in the Underglobe. Then there is the photograph on the stage and some of us will not come until April 2019.

David Bellwood is the access manager at the Globe. Each season there are performances that offer access to people who may find going to the theatre challenging. So, the SWP and the Globe make some performances easier to attend. Most plays have one that is being enhanced by British Sign Language, or one that provides captions on individual tablets. There are also, what is termed, "relaxed performances." These give audience members, who find an enclosed space a problem, more freedom to leave during the performance. We also look after their guide dogs. That is a much sought-after duty.

There is also a ramp available in the Globe for wheelchair-users, who would like to be in front of the actors in the yard. Another position is near the lift in the Gentlemen's Box. This

is slightly further from the stage, but a very comfortable place. I have taken a friend many times over there. One can even book a parking place near the stage door. She
was thrilled when some actors exited the door at the same time.

The summer season of 2019 saw some interesting changes at the Globe. There is now a resident Globe Ensemble. In previous years there were auditions each year, although some actors came back many times. Now there are eleven actors and two co-directors. It is similar to what the Shakespeare Company did 400 years ago. The ensemble will work together in Henry IV part 1 and 2 and Henry V. They will then perform in the Sam Wanamaker Playhouse (SWP) in Richard III and Henry VI part 2 and 3.

There were some days when the Globe presented the 3 Henry plays continuous. It was a great idea and I was tempted to steward these, but then accepted the fact that I did not have the energy any more for such a long day. Reluctantly, I worked the plays on different days. Some audience members had a problem too, especially the tourists. Many come to the Globe to get a look and feel of the place, but this is difficult if the play makes it a challenge. One did have to know some history to understand what the play was about. Sarah Amankwah played Hal and Henry. It is a demanding role, especially if the actor has to cope with the noisy environment. This is so different from the usual indoor theatre. There seemed to be an awful lot of planes during the first night's performance. It certainly provided a challenge for the actors who were on that open stage.

On the first performance of Henry IV, part 1, the programmes were given free, sponsored by Merian Global Investors who are now the principal sponsors of the Globe.

The other plays during the summer of 2019 were 'The Merry Wives of Windsor'. Pearce Quigley, who has been on the Globe stage many times, played Falstaff. I remember him from his part in 'Doctor Faustus' some years ago'.

In 'The Midsummer Night's Dream' Titania arrived in a decorated golf cart, driven through the crowded yard. It was amusing to see a wide gap appearing suddenly in a full yard. She then went to sleep in a decorated dustbin were Bottom joined her. It was great fun. Then the Touring Company came back after their travels to finish their performances at the Globe.

In the week before Christmas we had performances for the whole family. Jenifer Toksvig and Sandi Toksvig created 'Christmas Snow at the Globe'. The theatre was full of children, their parents and grandparents. The weather was typically English with rain and low temperatures. There was much audience participation and the word snow was mentioned by the children when asked what they hoped for. We had been asked to keep quiet about it, but there was snow (artificial) at the end of the performance. The children were delighted, and some adults too. This event was an enjoyable end to the 2019 season.

It had been a busy year for me. There were so many events in SWP during the summer and I did not want to miss these as they are often one-off performances. I divided my time between the 2 theatres as well as I could. Normally I give 100 duties in the summer, but this time I managed 50 in the Globe and 50 in the SWP. To my surprise, I received a certificate at the end-of-season party for giving so much time. It has been an enjoyable year. How lovely to be retired and choose what one wants to do.

80

Sam Wanamaker Playhouse

After the Sackler Gallery was opened and used for rehearsals, the spaces in the Globe building were available to create the indoor theatre that they were meant for. After the 2012 season, there were changes. The main stairs in the front entrance were enlarged. A cafe was put into the lower area on the left and the box office and information desk were put to the right. Shell for the new theatre had always been there. It was on three floors. Now it was going to be an indoor theatre on three floors.

On 20th October 2012, the Globe hired a coach to take some of us to Reading to see the timber frame and try out the seats. Peter McCurdy's firm was working on this. It would be transported to London, once it had been constructed. It was interesting sitting on these seats, but difficult to imagine what the real thing would be. The SWP is based on drawings discovered in Worcester College, Oxford. The Jacobean theatre is based on these drawings; but they can only provide so much information. The place will be lit by candle light from six chandeliers. There will be a pit and two galleries. The seats are wooden, but will be covered with cushions. Only in the back seats will one be able to lean, the others have no back. The seating is about 340. The doorways in the galleries have curtains with pictures of the muses. There is a corridor running all around the galleries.

The stewards had to be specially trained, as the duties were quite different. This was not easy for some. There were four doors on each level and one door into the pit area. The standing positions were numbered on the Upper Gallery. Each door had a steward there, who had to stand during the performance. In the first few weeks, the position was outside in the corridor and no seats could be put there as this was an evacuation route. It was not possible to leave this position and one had to wait for a break until the interval. The outside stewards were there for the whole performance. At first, the steward in the pit was meant to stand in the doorway. This became impractical as the actors used this route for exits and entrances. There was also a cloakroom, opposite the cafe, a first for the Globe. One of the steward's position was the cloakroom and they would not be able to see any plays during that time. I quite liked this duty sometimes, but many others did not. It was also difficult to stand for the entire first part of a play. Things became easier after a while. Just like in the Globe, it was seeing how to do matters in the best possible and safest way. This was changed later. The stewards could stand inside the doorway and if a seat next to them was empty they could sit there. The steward in the pit could sit on A1 or A6, it was the only designated sitting position in the SWP.

The candles were lit by a candle technician. The candles were doused during the interval and then lit again. If there was a lot of movement, they sometimes dripped. This could be painful. One visitor from abroad got wax on his shirt and instead of complaining, he said he would take it home and keep it as a souvenir.

Like in the Globe, there was a musician's gallery over the stage, and seats could be sold there if they were not needed for the actors.

The SWP was so different to the Globe. It also meant that we would now be needed all year round. At least we would not have to worry about the weather. We would not have to wear noisy rustling macs.

Another bonus was, that light could be used with more imaginative purposes. There was electric light in the corridors and the colour could be changed to add to the atmosphere. The windows had shutters that could be left open or closed to add to this. Actors could use that space to create sounds and speak from a distance.

The first play in the SWP was 'The Duchess of Malfi' by John Webster. Dominic Dromgoole was the Director and

Gemma Arterten played the Duchess. As there were 340 seats, it was easily sold out. People were not familiar with the best seats and it was an experiment for them where to sit. There are pillars and therefore restricted-view-seats. There is little room for luggage, hence the cloakroom. As a short person, I find the pit tiring as I need to look up a lot. People tend not to faint in the SWP as much as in the Globe, but there is an FA on every level.

Eileen Atkins did a one-man show, being Ellen Terry. It was so well-liked, that it was brought back. 'The Knight of the Burning Pestle' by Francis Beaumont was next. It was interesting to see the reaction of the audience who did not know the play. Two actors came and sat among them, opened a rustling paper bag with sweets and offered some to the people around them. It was really funny. As there were only 340 seats, it was easily sold out.

This Jacobean theatre was made for plays that were not often seen. There was: 'The Changeling' (by Middleton and Rowley), 'Tis a Pity She's a Whoré' by Ford, the 'Broken Heart' by Ford and 'Dido, Queen of Carthage' by Marlowe. Because of my long time at the Globe, I had seen all the Shakespeare plays and some of them many times. Now I was ready for something else. I did not know that there was such a wealth of material from bygone days. I had such an enjoyable time.

15/08/2018

The Royal Opera House brought a small company to perform 'L'Ormindo'. The music is by Francesco Cavalli and the libretto is by Giovanni Faustini. It was enchanting. The SWP has very good acoustics with all that wood around and the real candles make it very special. There were so many music events on weekends and I stewarded as many as I could get.

If I was not needed, I bought a ticket and stood in the Upper Gallery. The tickets for standing were £10. It was not necessary to see the musicians performing, it was more import to hear them.

But it was not only classical music. There were unusual events like 'The Rubber-Bandits'. The seats were taken out of the pit and the audience could dance and join in. These events brought their followers and were lively evenings of fun. At the beginning of the SWP, photography was not permitted and customers were very disappointed not to be allowed to take a picture of this beautiful, unusual place. This rule was changed later, and it was like the Globe; photography was permitted during the in-coming and the interval, just not when the actors or musicians were on stage. This rule was relaxed during the 'Rubber- Bandits' to the delight of the fans.

Now we had so many musicians who came again and again. I was in my element. Shakespeare's plays had been a passion and this was put on hold for a while, perhaps until the next summer season.

In February 2015, Mark Rylance came to the SWP. The composer, Claire van Kampen, had written a play about the Spanish King Philippe V, who was cured with the help of an Italian castrato. This was a great play with Mark's acting and some excellent singing. It did so well that it moved to the West End.

In October 2015, Shakespeare plays came again. It was Dominic's last year at the Globe and he put on the four last plays by Shakespeare: Pericles, Cymbeline, The Winter's Tale and The Tempest. My joy in Shakespeare's language came back. I worked at the SWP that season for over 100 performances and it was a delight. There was another play that was memorable: 'Comus' by John Milton. The pillars had heads of gargoyles and a Green Man looking down. At the end of that season, I happened to exit through the stage door. Looking up, I saw these figures hanging on the balcony. I asked a stage hand whether I could buy one and was told I could have one. I choose the Green Man. He came home with me on the train and now graces a wall in my garden. He has found a good home.

When I started at the Globe in 1995, I had not imagined that my life would be so enriched by the activities there. In 2016 in the SWP, we had 'All the Angels' by Nick Drake. It was about Handel and the first performance of the Messiah. David Horovitch played Handel and I felt that Handel had been like that. A friend of mine is writing a book about Handel and I encouraged him to come and listen to this play.

There were too many plays and I enjoyed all of them, especially when I stewarded them from different positions. I spend a lot of time at the SWP in the winter. But then there were some very exciting new things happening there, in the summer as well. I had to divide my time between the Globe and the SWP. To my surprise, I managed to do an equal number in each theatre. As I am getting more advanced in years, I do not work two shifts in one day anymore, I choose the evening productions.

There are a few plays I would like to mention and apologise for those I do not. This is not because I forgot those, or did not like them. There are just too many to fit into this book. How lucky I was to come to England to learn English. It changed my life and made it richer than I could have envisaged in 1958.

Here are a few plays I will mention. 'The Four Seasons', with music by Vivaldi. It was in the traditional Japanese form of bunrakku. There were puppets and music, but no words. It was enchanting and appreciated by many. 'The Flying Lovers of Vitebsk' by Daniel Jamieson was about Marc Chagall, an artist I admired since I saw his work at the Royal Academy. I also visited the church in Tudeley, a small village in Kent, where there are some windows he designed. This was a commission by a parent, whose daughter died at sea. There are concerts held in that church which gives one ample opportunity to look at the beautiful blue windows.

Plays in the Sam Wanamaker Playhouse (SWP)

The Royal Opera House came back in 2015 to give us: 'Orpheus', music by Luigi Rossi and the libretto by Francesco Buti. It is a joy to hear music by candlelight. There was so much music in the SWP that I spent much time there. If I could not get a shift, or I wanted to make sure I would be inside a performance, I bought a ticket. I was usually standing. The view from this position is not ideal for a play, but for music, one can hear very well from any place. There were too many concerts for me to mention. Some musicians came back each year and tickets for these were sold very quickly.

Jessica Swale wrote 'Thomas Tallis'. There is not that much known about him and this gave her an opportunity to invent. The Sixteen sung for us and it was a joy to listen.

Nick Drake wrote: 'All the Angels: Handel and the First Messiah'. I loved these performances and David Horovitch was, to me, just as I imagined Handel had been.

The Carducci String Quartet gave us 'The Complete Quartets by Shostakovich'. It started at 11 am and finished just before 10 pm. I was there the whole day and I felt privileged to be able to do this. We also had poetry. Julian Glover adapted and introduced 'Beowulf'.

Derek Walcott gave us 'Omeros'. It was performed by Joan Iyiola and Joseph Marcell with music played by Tayo Akinbode. I did stand on the shores and gazed at the horizon, listening to the breakers, just as the programme suggested.

In 2015, there were six evenings called 'Winter's Tales'. These were read by Penelope Wilton, Deborah Findlay, Roger Allum, Aidan Gillen, James Norton and Harriet Walter. The tales were by Chekhov, Mansfield, D.H. Lawrence, James Joyce, Fitzgerald and Du Maurier. It was a very popular event and many of us hoped it would be repeated. We are still waiting patiently.

Lucy Bailey produced 'Comus', a masque by John Milton. It is very different from Shakespeare and only 25 pages long. It combines lyric poetry and drama and lends itself to dance and music. The gargoyles hanging from the pillars were effective and I was lucky to get permission to take the Green

Man home. He is now hanging in my garden and appreciated by many neighbours.

'The Little Matchgirl' from the Hans Christian Andersen stories, came to the SWP. It started with Thumbelina being homeless and looking for warmth. She meets a mouse, a toad, a swallow, beetles and a prince. The role was connected by the character, 'Ole Shuteye', played by Paul Hunter. Fairy Tales are also appreciated by grown-ups and I am one of them. I asked to buy the puppet but it was kept for other performances and did come back a year later. There were changes in the cast, but Edie Edmundson was the handler again.

'The White Devil' by John Webster is a plot full of twists. It is like a riddle: Who is the White Devil? Discussions in the stewards' room gave a variety of characters and how can a devil be white? A sermon published after the first performance in the 16th century, was called: 'The White Devil' or 'The Hypocrite', "Encased and condemned those who hid their inner voices behind a show of virtue."

Sometimes plays on the Globe stage were transferred to the SWP. It was interesting to see how the smaller and intimate theatre gave a new look to the productions. Othello was one of these and some audience members found it hard to be so close to the murder.

'All's Well That Ends Well', is sometimes seen as a problem comedy. This may be because Helena is determined to marry Bertram. She does so, but if we think about it 'How will it work'? This play fitted well onto the small stage at the SWP. One felt to be so much closer to the characters and their actions.

Anders Lustgarten wrote 'The Secret Theatre'. It is a play about Francis Walsingham and his spy networks. There was some more history for me to become familiar with. I am taking a great interest in this subject and wish I had more time to read further details. The story is firmly set in the 1580s.

John Dryden's play, 'Aurang-zeb', was published in 1676. It was directed by Barrie Rutter and performed in the SWP as 'The Captive Queen', in association with Northern Broadsides. It was Rutter's last production with Broadsides. He liked rhyming couplets and for me, it was a change to hear a play in that way.

John Wolfson wrote 'The Inn at Lydda'. It gives a meeting between Caesar and Christ, although the two never met. But there were twelve Caesar's and they were powerful men. This play has many characters and many places where an action takes place.

In 2018, there were many talks and plays dealing with Shakespeare and race. Tanika Gupta wrote a play about his grandfather's youngest brother, Dinesh Gupta. Dinesh wrote about 92 letters from prison. He was imprisoned because he was a rebel. He threw shoes at men who beat their wives. He did not think this should happen. The play was called 'The Lions and the Tigers'. The lions were the British and the tigers were the Bengalis. It was very moving.

We also had a talk by Keith Hamilton Cobb. He was a black man who played Othello. His feelings were different from those of the producer and he told us about these. He said that a producer needed to think how these perspectives influenced the acting. At the exhibition in the British Library, 'Shakespeare in Ten Acts', act six talks about Ira Aldridge, the first black actor to play Othello. He did this at the Theatre Royal in Covent Garden and he provoked a racist campaign in the press for daring to speak the words of the English national poet. And to do so in one of England's national theatres. This relationship between Shakespeare and the politics of race, resonates even now.

'Romantics Anonymous', is a story about chocolate and shyness. I know about both. I grew up as an only child and I am very shy and find it difficult even now to join in, preferring the company of books. A nice touch before this play was that everyone was given a piece of chocolate. Carly Bawden went to a chocolate factory to learn the art of making chocolate. The story was about two people who were both very shy and met through a love of chocolate. The play started with Carly stirring a mixture and singing to herself. The Globe shop sold boxes of chocolates modelled on the boxes shown in the play.

During the Festival of Independence, a play by Vijay Tendulkar was shown. It had been performed in India in 1981 and created a stir. It is a revolutionary one and deals with a complex love triangle taking place on a college campus. The topic deals with same-sex love and is still taboo. It is a thought-provoking story that showed this in a sensitive way. It should be performed more often.

Usually during the summer months, the SWP is used for education events. In 2017, there were so many events, often one-off and I could not resist stewarding as many as possible. For the first time, I managed an equal number of duties in the Globe and in the SWP. I was in my element keeping up with all the actions and trying not to miss anything.

The season in 2018 started with 'Macbeth'. Michelle Terry played Lady Macbeth and Paul Ready, her real-life husband' played Macbeth. I have seen many productions of this play, but this really spoke to me. I worked it 20 times and saw it from all angles in the SWP. To me, it emphasised the fact that Lady Macbeth was guiltier than her husband. Then I found the book, Macbeth, by Jo Nesbo, a commission using the story of Macbeth and putting it in contemporary times. I read this on the train to the theatre and then stewarded the play. I saw so much more and I looked forward to it each time. Then we had a talk in the Nancy Knowles Theatre by Emma Smith. She pointed out so many details and the story became even clearer to me. Unfortunately, one of the audience members became unwell and I looked after her and missed the second half of the talk. That is part of being a steward and a FA, and I accept it. Do I want to see a performance of Macbeth ever again? Sometimes when I have been to a play that I really enjoyed I try not to see it again, but keep it in my memory as the definite.

Oliver Chris compiled, edited and dramatised 'Ralegh: The Treason Trial'. The SWP stage was set up as a court room. Some 12 members from the audience were given the role as the jury. During the interval, they went to a room to discuss the case and came back to give their verdict. Two stewards became jury stewards and wore black gowns. The jurors had been contacted before the play and asked if they wanted to take this part. How versatile the SWP is.

In 2011, the Globe Theatre gave 'Doctor Faustus' on the large stage. Now it was offered at the SWP. I do like that play and have read the German version by Goethe, which is different, but has similar ideas. I wondered how the play would work on a smaller stage. The first surprise was that Dr Faustus, was a woman and played by Jocelyn Jee Esien. Mephistopheles, was also a woman and was played by Pauline McLynn. I was not disappointed by these changes. I loved the play as much as I had loved the earlier version in the Globe. The scene at the end, when Faustus reflects on his life was very moving and I admired Jocelyn for making it so, I stewarded it 15 times.

How does the myth of Doctor Faustus speak to a woman? Little has been written about this. The Globe commissioned some writers to deal with this question and five short plays were performed after the play. They lasted 30 minutes each. All five were also shown in succession a few times, once in the tiring house. The title was: 'Dark Night of the Soul'.

Lily Bevan wrote 'The French Welcome' based on Shakespeare's stay with the Mountjoy's in Silver Street.

Katie Hims wrote 'Three Minutes after Midnight'. Her niece is waiting for her sister to die and a secret is revealed.

Rachael Spence and Lisa Hammond wrote 'Souled Out'; this asked the question, 'Do we have a soul?'

Athena Stevens' play was 'Recompense'. Twenty-five years ago, a life was changed 'through human error'.

Amanda Wilkins wrote 'The little Sob'. Are we willing to tell the truth or do we hide and admit that we did nothing?

Each of these short plays gave a different aspect about women dealing with a situation. It provided much thought and encouraged conversation.

Edward II was the play by Marlowe. It dealt with the relationship of the King and Gaveston. I had never seen this play before and not knowing much history, the content was new to me. I felt the production treated the subject with sensitivity. Of course, the attitude towards homosexuality has changed much and today's audience watches it with different perspectives.

Richard II was an all-female performance by actors of different colours. The playhouse showed large photographs of the ancestors of the actors and all the people involved in the production These looked down at them from the balcony. The actors wore costumes of their country and nationality. If one became involved in the play it was easy to become engrossed in the action and forget the differences in gender and nationality. Richard was played by Adjoa Andoh. The final scene is so emotional and my admiration for the actress playing it night after night with such feeling.

'After Edward' is written by Tom Stuart. He is an actor and has performed at the Globe and the SWP. The central character is Edward who is dropped onto the stage and meets Gertrude Stein, Harvey Milk and Quentin Crisp, people who were open about their sexuality. They helped, in their time, to open up discussion about this. The audience of today looks at this subject with more understanding. It was some thought-provoking performances.

'Bartholomew Fair' by Ben Johnson is a comedy that has 30 characters. This means many changes of costumes, especially at the SWP. It was a challenge to work out who was playing who. Most of the seats in the pit had been removed and only the back row was left, but there had to be a steward. It felt strange sitting among 21 people, and I enjoyed it.

Some years ago, the Education Department gave us some talks about 'Shakespeare is German'. This year they looked at Poland's affinity with the Bard. It is the 150th anniversary of the birth of the Polish playwright, painter, designer and interpreter of Shakespeare, Stanislaus Wyspianski. We saw 'Death of Ophelia' in the SWP. The programme had a beautiful painting of 'God the Father' on the cover of the programme. It was a memorable evening. In the 16th century the German Schiegel argued that Shakespeare was German. The Polish festival in 2019 can also say that Shakespeare was Polish. There were a few one-off events in the SWP. One was an evening of reading two works by Virginia Woolf, 'A Room of One's Own' and 'Three Guineas'. It was sold out and the audience appreciated the event. It is difficult to judge how long such a reading will last and, as often happens, people who need to catch a train have to miss the ending.

Hearing books read in a theatre seems to be a new venture. We also had a few evenings to listen to ghost stories. The theatre was kept very dark and one actor stood on the stage. It was quite unearthly. I stewarded this and thought with apprehension, what would I do if an audience member was overcome by the story. Everyone seemed to be engrossed and all was well.

Richard III has started in the SWP. I have worked it 25 times and I am still seeing something new each time. My first duty was in the Upper Gallery, and as we as stewards have to stand back, I did not see much of the play. I could hear it though, and I listened with appreciation to the words. I loved this production from that moment. There were some interesting touches. The stage was covered with a mount of soil. Richard was played by a woman, Sophie Russell. There were no physical disfigurations. The whole experience, for me, was so exciting and I looked forwards to more duties. I have seen it from all angles and I am still watching it.

Ella Hickson has written 'Swive' (Elizabeth). There are four actors, two women and two men. Two actors play Elizabeth, one as a young princess and one as a Queen. It shows how she managed to survive as the first unmarried Queen. The performance lasts 90 minutes without an interval. The theatre is kept dark and movement in the audience is kept to a minimum. The actors talk in a relaxed way, with pauses between thoughts. It gives a different atmosphere and the SWP is just the place to do such a work. I loved it from the first time I saw it.

Another play performed by the Globe Ensemble is Henry VI, part 2 and 3. It takes three hours and has two intervals. That is unusual for performances at the Globe and SWP. For me it is history backwards. Richard III is before Henry VI, but I saw Richard first. I have now seen Henry VI and it ends with the mount of earth, which is the start of Richard. Gradually, the gaps in history are filled in for me. I know, Shakespeare takes liberties when he writes the plays, but it does give me some idea of it.

The Sam Wanamaker Playhouse is an exciting and intimate theatre. Normally, its season starts after the Globe has finished in the summer. In 2019 however, there were many plays and events in the SWP during the summer. I was torn between which one to steward, and I was not the only one.

The Globe

The theatre is called "Shakespeare's Globe Theatre, London." On a few occasions someone turned up with a ticket for the Shakespeare Theatre in Stratford-upon-Avon. The Globe is now really one of the frequent places visited in London. We also have stewards coming from America and Germany to work at the Globe for a few weeks each year. The German steward brings a group of students, does some duties and returns home. He does this a few times each year. The students all speak English well, but I often point out to them that Shakespeare's English is different and they should listen to it more.

The first Artistic Director at the Globe was Mark Rylance. He is an actor and looked at the place from an actor's point of view. He liked the stage to stay as it was, no extensions and very few props. There were two companies of actors, the red and the white. There was no permanent company and auditions happened each year. The actors had to be able to cope with helicopters, pigeons and noisy audience members. They had to project well in that open space. We could always tell who had been there before, as they could be heard. They all had their own way of warming up. Mark started a game of yard ball. There were definite rules and it looked like a great game. Stewards were not allowed to join in, but we sometimes had to retrieve the ball from the galleries.

At first there were two Shakespeare plays and two by contemporary authors. Each company showed the Shakespeare play and rehearsed the other one. Mark was good at including the audience, planes and birds. It would not have done to stop and wait for the noise to go. Sometimes people became unwell and we had to help them out. If this was not easy, Mark used to indicate with his little finger that the play should stop. The actors paused and waited for a signal to start again. If we stewarded a play, several times we noticed subtle the changes. This was probably to keep the play from becoming stale. I used to watch with interest and notice these variations.

The yard tickets were £5 and many people came again and again, standing in front of the stage and watching each move. They also noticed the changes and the stewards got to know the regulars.

Mark also liked to bless the stage at the beginning of the season. Water was taken from the Thames and sprinkled around the stage. One year a Swami came and brought a small bottle of water from the Ganges. This was mixed with the Thames water and taken around the stage.

Mark also took the Globe players to other places. The first one was in 2002 when they performed 'Twelfth Night' at Middle Temple Hall. It was to remember the 2nd February in 1602 when this play had taken place there. The audience walked past the open dressing rooms and observed the actors putting on their makeup. Mark introduced this later at the Globe as it was much appreciated by the audience. The stewards were needed at Middle Temple and although I was still working, I managed to do a few. Mulled Wine was served and snacks of manchets, kickshaws and cracknels were given out. The music was performed in the balcony and consisted of a broken consort. This was a combination of the cittern of the barber shop, the violin of taverns, the flute with its military association and the viol, lute and oak-leafed shaped bandora of more polite society. The Masters of Music were Claire van Kampen and Keith McGowan. The Globe went back to Middle Temple Hall a few times, and I stewarded these several times.

In 2004, the Globe decided to take three plays to Hampton Court. It was in recognition of 1603 when the new King's Men were invited to entertain James I, at his first Christmas in England.

There were also a few productions at some of the Inns of Court. The lawyers have an amateur drama group and they invited the Globe to perform in their halls and churches. There was a memorable production at Gray's Inn. No artificial light was used. The performance of King John started in the afternoon and the natural light added to the atmosphere as the day came to an end. I tried very hard to get a duty and as these events usually took place at weekends, I was lucky and managed to get a duty.

Mark Rylance decided to do other things and after 10 years at the Globe, left. He gave a tea party for all the stewards who had started with him. He knew all of us and was always ready to greet us with a smile. His wife, Claire van Kampen, provided Elizabethan music and also got to know us. Mark had tried so many things, all male and all female productions, old and new costumes, authentic pronunciation, etc. It was an innovative 10 years.

Dominic Dromgoole was the second Artistic Director. He started in 2006. I was looking forward to seeing some changes, and we got them; it was exciting. Dominic liked extending the stage into the yard. This was a bonus for the audience, as there was now more opportunity to rest their elbows on the wood. He also increased the number of plays and the season became longer. There were quite a few new plays and I have mentioned these in a previous chapter.

The Globe did not only do plays, there were a variety of other events. The Comedy Store comes once each year. It brings in a different audience and the place sounds different. There have also been two evenings of 'The Alternative Miss

World'. Photography was allowed and the party after in the Underglobe goes on well into the night. The BBC recorded '500 Words' and our duty started at 5am. This was the same for the children and parents. Recordings usually have long pauses and it was challenging for all of us. The children who had won their category, had their story read by well-known people and the Duchess of Cornwall gave a speech. It was a long day for all of us. I worked all of these one-off events as I also like variety. There were the usual comments that this theatre should stick to Shakespeare. I think he would have liked it and probably written a play about it. We shall never know, but it is interesting and gives opportunities for discussions.

We also had pop concerts where the stage was filled with musical instruments and other props. A far cry from the days of Elizabethan concerts. There were a few of those in the pre-season, but they did not fill the space. There was a full orchestra on stage, to provide the music when we saw a film about Joan of Arc.

During Dominic Dromgoole's time, we had Shakespeare's 37 plays, each in a different language. He took a company all over the world performing 'Hamlet' in a variety of venues and countries. He also created 'The Complete Walk'. In 2014, the Sam Wanamaker Theatre was opened. The last four plays by Shakespeare were performed. I realised how much I had learnt and I worked over 100 duties. It was a delight.

The third Artistic Director was a woman, Emma Rice. She liked music and movement and wanted to attract a new audience of young people who did not feel Shakespeare was for them. This sounds a bit like me, years ago. Amplification and lights were installed. Tables were put in the yard for actors to jump on and off. When checking tickets at the glass doors, we often heard "I am a Newbie."

Many of the actors had not worked at the Globe and they had a challenging time coping with the helicopters and pigeons. Again, it emphasised how different this place is to other theatres.

Artificial trees with sparkling lights were put on the piazza and the riverside. The lights were magical at night and the trees provided a welcome seating area.

The dress code for the stewards changed. We were given turquoise t-shirts and a choice of either turquoise or pink sweatshirts. This had to be combined with black or white lower garments.

Michelle Terry became our next Artistic Director. She is an actress and has performed several times at the Globe. I remember her as the Princess of France in 'Love's Labour's Lost' when the stage had a triangular extension. Only 20 people were allowed in this with a steward. The audience had to remain in this space as continuous movement would have been too disruptive.

Of course. It was a favourite position. I brought some young friends and they enjoyed it so much that they actually wanted to see more Shakespeare. That play ended with a fight, using baguettes. The pigeons queued up for the crumps before the audience had left.

Michelle started her season with 'Hamlet', playing the title role. Mark Rylance came back to the Globe and played Iago in 'Othello'.

I have written about the plays in the Globe and the plays in the SWP in previous chapters.

The Shakespeare Authorship Trust

This SAT meets once a year at the Globe, usually in October or November. Members spend all day discussing, "Who wrote Shakespeare?" They come with slides and notes and books, talking about their new discoveries of who wrote all these plays. I doubt if there ever will be a definite answer, but there is much fun talking and thinking about it. So many people work enthusiastically on this question.

The SAT is like an exciting club, you are either in it or not. Whenever the topic is mentioned, the discussion starts. I am often throwing up the question in the stewards' room as I enjoy encouraging controversy. It is just fun to do this.

The most often mentioned names of possible authors, instead of Shakespeare, are Francis Bacon, Christopher Marlowe and the Earl of Oxford. There are a few names that come up occasionally and Queen Elizabeth is one of them. Sometimes a new name springs up and a whole new set of books appear on the subject.

For over 200 years, nobody doubted that Shakespeare was the author. Then someone voiced the opinion that a glove maker's son could not have known so many topics and the debate started. More than 5,000 books have been written about this and quite a few names have come up. This is an ongoing event and I enjoy being part of it. It will keep many writers busy for a very long time.

I enjoy this day and have stewarded it each year. It is interesting to listen to the pros and cons. Speakers bring books they have written and there is a book table. That is my favourite position and I have got to know the regular speakers. I would never have thought about this subject when I started stewarding at the Globe. Now I am enjoying the debates, but do not know enough to give a positive answer,

There are refreshments during the day and a cake at the end of it. All this is organised by Bronwyn Robertson. It takes a lot of work and she makes it an enjoyable day.

25 Years

It is now 25 years since I walked into Bear Gardens. It was the office of Shakespeare's Globe Theatre. A large bear was standing in the entrance.

I was there to apply to become a volunteer for the Globe. That building was not yet finished, but part of it gave an idea of what it would be like. It was a baby that was developing.

My English had improved and I was now ready to learn about Shakespeare. What a journey this was. I was still working as a teacher and my spare time was limited. There was so much to learn. It was not only the plays, but all the works that had been written about these plays.

I started slowly and volunteered only at weekends. This made it possible for me to steward some of the events provided by a very busy education department. I was learning along students and this helped. Some of my own pupils attended these workshops and it encouraged me to talk about this during my lessons.

In 1995, it was still possible to drive in London and to find parking places. This made it easy for me to get to Blackfriars and get home in reasonable time. When I retired in 2000, I got my freedom pass. I started using the train to and from London Bridge. The walk from there to the Globe was through a derelict part, but that was no problem for me. I could read on the train there and back and this helped me to wind down after the shift. When the train service to and from Blackfriars started to run, I used that, as I could walk to my local station. The walk along the river after a performance was very relaxing.

The Globe Theatre started slowly with four plays a season and some educational events. Then there were more plays and the education department provided so much more. At first, I was able to give around 30 duties. Once I retired, I came more often and my duties came to around a 100 in the theatre and some 20 or so connected with education.

The theatre had grown and was now a teenager. The demand for rooms increased and the education department increased. The building in Bear Gardens was demolished and the Sackler was built. This provided more rehearsal rooms and offices. There was also a cafe for the public. Then more space was needed again and the activities grew. So, fund-raising started for further building work, the Prospero, and it is hoped to have enough to start with that project soon. Sam Wanamaker's idea, had been a Shakespeare Complex that would always grow and never stop.

The site of the Globe Theatre also needed more space. There was now an exhibition open to visitors. The tour guides provided a talk and a visit to the theatre. The shop increased its merchandise. The costume department wanted more space. The workshop made more scenery and needed more equipment to put it up and perhaps store it. The steward numbers grew and they needed more lockers and chairs to get ready for their shift. The number of staff working in the offices grew and they needed desks and computers. That place is so crowded now that I lose my way in it, every time I have to go there. The library wanted a special place to keep their collections and to display these. The demand for space is never-ending.

Then the Sam Wanamaker Playhouse opened in 2014 after months of construction work. The shell had always been within the original building. Now it needed to be fitted with air-conditioning, lights and seating. The foyer had to be changed to make it easy for the increased number of people expected. The Box Office got a prime position near the entrance. There is now an information desk near the doors to deal with the many questions that the visitors have. The Friend's desk was moved nearer the shop. The bar, now called 'The Swan', was enlarged.

There was continuous maintenance in the theatre. The roof needed to be re-thatched. The magpies seem to think it was done for them to find more food under the moss. The décor in the Gentlemen's Rooms was renewed and large paintings of the Muses were put on the walls. Both theatres continued to grow.

On 24th March 2019, I stewarded a performance by Harrow School. It was their anniversary of 25 years on the Globe stage. They had performed 'Twelfth Night' in 1994 and this was their anniversary. The weather was kind to us, if a little cold. The audience were mostly parents and friends. The performance was extremely good and the students were so talented. On 27th March 2019, I shall work the last performance of the school's play, 'Romeo and Juliet', which is sponsored by Deutsche Bank.

It has been an amazing time for me stewarding all these years. In 2019 I worked 70 performances in the SWP and 16 for the schools since October. There will be fewer for me now as I have stopped doing double duties and only come to evening performances. It is easier for me to steward in the winter months. The summer is busy with playing croquet.